Building the
WHITE HOUSE

By Benjamin Proudfit

Gareth Stevens
PUBLISHING

Please visit our website, www.garethstevens.com. For a free color catalog of all our high-quality books, call toll free 1-800-542-2595 or fax 1-877-542-2596.

Library of Congress Cataloging-in-Publication Data

Proudfit, Benjamin.
Building the White House / by Benjamin Proudfit.
p. cm. — (What you didn't know about history)
Includes index.
ISBN 978-1-4824-1930-6 (pbk.)
ISBN 978-1-4824-1929-0 (6-pack)
ISBN 978-1-4824-1931-3 (library binding)
1. White House (Washington, D.C.) — Juvenile literature. 2. Washington (D.C.) — Buildings, structures, etc. — Juvenile literature. I. Title.
F204.W5 P76 2015
975.3—d23

First Edition

Published in 2015 by
Gareth Stevens Publishing
111 East 14th Street, Suite 349
New York, NY 10003

Designer: Andrea Davison-Bartolotta
Editor: Kristen Rajczak

Photo credits: Cover, p. 1 Fotosearch/Getty Images; p. 5 (inset) blinkblink/Shutterstock.com; p. 5 (main) Globe Turner/Shutterstock.com; pp. 7 (main), 9 Benjamin Henry Latrobe/LOC.gov; p. 7 (inset) Buyenlarge/Getty Images; pp. 8, 13 courtesy of LOC.gov; p. 10 Keystone-France/Gemma-Keystone via Getty Images; p. 11 William Strickland/LOC.gov; p. 12 www.whitehousemuseum.org; p. 15 Abbie Rowe/National Archives and Records Administration/Wikimedia Commons; p. 16 Ed Clark/Time Life Pictures/Getty Images; p. 17 (inset) Dmitri Kessel/Time Life Pictures/Getty Images; p. 17 (main) FPG/Getty Images; p. 19 Harry S. Truman Library/National Archives and Records Administration; p. 20 Bill Clark/Roll Call/Getty Images; p. 21 Vacclav/Shutterstock.com.

Printed in the United States of America

CPSIA compliance information: Batch #CW15GS: For further information contact Gareth Stevens, New York, New York at 1-800-542-2595.

CONTENTS

Words in the glossary appear in **bold** type the first time they are used in the text.

FROM THE BEGINNING

The story of building the White House starts more than 200 years ago, soon after the United States won its freedom from England. George Washington became president in 1789, and Congress let him choose where the capital—and the president's **mansion**—would be.

But the story of the White House is as much about rebuilding as building! Major changes and additions have occurred several times since the original construction. Some presidents built up, while others built out. A movie theater, bowling alley, and pools have been built, too!

Did You Know?

President George Washington lived in three houses while he was president—the White House wasn't one of them. Two were in New York City, and one was in Philadelphia, Pennsylvania.

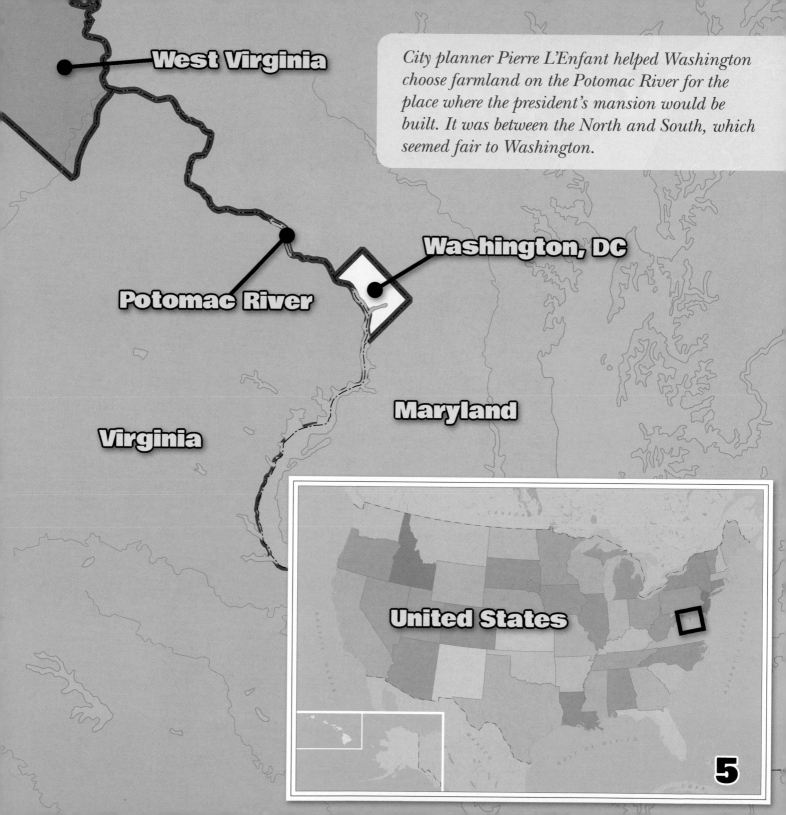

West Virginia

City planner Pierre L'Enfant helped Washington choose farmland on the Potomac River for the place where the president's mansion would be built. It was between the North and South, which seemed fair to Washington.

Washington, DC

Potomac River

Maryland

Virginia

United States

5

TRULY WHITE

Thomas Jefferson had the idea to have a contest to **design** the president's mansion. Nine **architects** presented plans. Washington chose a simple design from an Irishman named James Hoban. It was based on the Leinster House in Dublin, Ireland. They look a lot alike!

Construction on the president's mansion began in 1792. The outside of the building was sandstone. Stone workers brought in from Scotland used a whitewash to seal the sandstone, making the president's mansion white!

Did You Know?

The cornerstone of the White House was set in 1792, but no one took note of where it was laid. To this day, no one knows where the original cornerstone is!

LEINSTER HOUSE, DUBLIN, 1792

Many buildings around the president's mansion were brick, so the white of the mansion was noticeable. The mansion wasn't commonly known as the White House until about 1817, though.

LIVABLE, BUT NOT DONE

When President John Adams moved into the White House in 1800, it wasn't finished. There was a hole where the grand staircase was supposed to go! **Plaster** on the walls was still wet—and about half of the rooms hadn't been plastered at all.

There's a story about Abigail Adams hanging the president's **laundry** in the East Room. She did, partly because she didn't think his laundry should be on view. But it was also because the room wasn't ready to use for anything else!

the White House from above, 1857

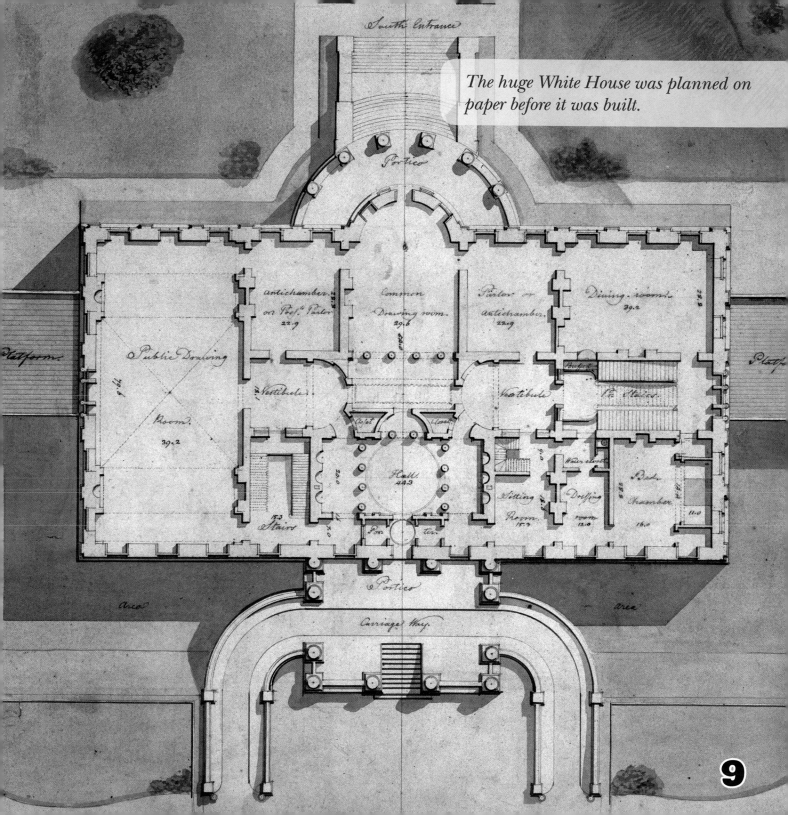

The huge White House was planned on paper before it was built.

9

FIRE!

Though the White House looks much as it did when it was built 200 years ago, the only parts of the structure that remain from that time are the outside stone walls. In 1814, the British set fire to both the White House and the Capitol building! They were **retaliating** for a US attack on the city of York in British-held Canada.

President James Madison and First Lady Dolley Madison made it out in time. However, the inside of the White House was ruined.

Did You Know?

Another fire damaged parts of the White House on December 24, 1929.

This picture shows how the White House looked after the fire according to one artist. President Madison wanted the mansion to look the same as it had before the fire to show that the US government wasn't easily beaten.

A BIG ADDITION

Until Theodore Roosevelt became president, the president's office was on the second floor of the White House, among the First Family's rooms. This created a problem as visitors to the president were so close to the First Family. Roosevelt had an additional problem. He had six children—his office offered no privacy!

Roosevelt began construction on offices for the president and staff in 1902. The West Wing, as the building would be called, was connected to the Family Residence by a walkway.

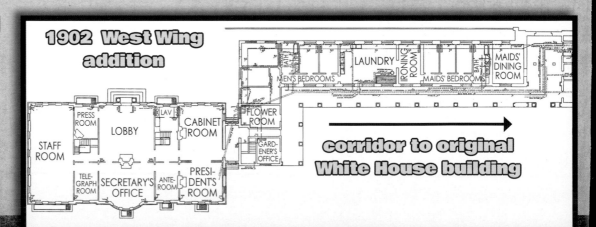

The West Wing, shown here, was originally called the Executive Office Building. In 1949, its name was changed to the West Wing officially.

Did-You-Know?

The president's office was originally rectangular! It was President William Howard Taft who built the first Oval Office. It was moved to its present position near the Rose Garden by President Franklin D. Roosevelt.

13

THE OVERHAUL

In 1948, the leg of a piano fell through the floor of one of the White House bedrooms. President Harry Truman had the rest of the mansion **evaluated**—and it was in pretty bad shape. Once again, the inside of the White House was almost totally rebuilt. The president even had to move out!

The original walls were kept, as was the third floor, but concrete and steel were added to support the building. Bulldozers dug deeper basements. Additionally, bathrooms were added to every bedroom!

Did You Know?

Renovations made by President Theodore Roosevelt and President Calvin Coolidge were partly to blame for the structural problems the White House faced by the time Truman was president.

When the renovations were finished in 1952, President Truman moved back in. The White House had been fireproofed and strengthened, but still looked like the American **symbol** it is.

There's much more to the building of the White House than just making more room or strengthening the walls. Each president has added little touches to bring the mansion up to the present day. President Thomas Jefferson took office in 1801 when the White House was still being completed. He added indoor water closets, which are somewhat like bathrooms.

In 1835, running water and central heating were added to the White House. Electric lighting followed in 1891.

Did You Know?

While she was First Lady from 1961 to 1963, Jacqueline Kennedy worked on **preserving** and displaying the historic **furnishings** of the house. She had the White House declared a museum, too.

President Franklin D. Roosevelt often needed a wheelchair to get around. He made changes to the White House to make this possible. This picture shows him wearing leg braces, which helped him walk.

White House pool built by President Franklin D. Roosevelt

17

THE COOLEST ADD-ONS

What else has been built into the White House? Here are just a few cool examples:

- In 1942, an East Wing addition was partly built to cover a bomb shelter! This safe room exists today as the Presidential Emergency Operations Center.

- President Theodore Roosevelt added a coatroom during his 1902 renovation. It's a movie theater now!

- Bowling lanes were first added to the White House in 1947 for President Truman's birthday. Those were moved to a different building a few years later. In 1969, President Richard Nixon added a new bowling lane.

This photograph from 1948 shows President Truman's bowling lanes at the White House. Strangely, Truman didn't even really like to bowl!

Did You Know?
The White House's windows are all bulletproof.

When President George Washington oversaw White House construction, he knew the building needed to be able to grow and change to fit the times. Today, that mostly means maintaining the building. During the early 1990s, the outside of the White House was redone. About 40 layers of paint were scraped off, and the whole building was repainted!

The White House is more than just a building. It's a symbol of freedom and needs to be preserved as an important part of US history.

Did You Know?

Each First Family is allowed to decorate their floors of the White House as they want.

White House Timeline

1792 — The cornerstone is laid for the White House.

1800 — President John Adams becomes the first to live in the White House.

1814 — A fire damages the inside of the White House.

1817 — The rebuilding of the White House is complete.

1902 — Construction of the West Wing begins under President Theodore Roosevelt.

1927 — President Coolidge turns the White House attic into a third floor.

1929 — A fire in the West Wing causes some damage.

1948 — President Harry Truman begins a huge renovation of the White House.

1952 — The Truman renovation is finished.

1961 — First Lady Jacqueline Kennedy begins her efforts to repair and preserve parts of the White House and its furnishings.

21

GLOSSARY

architect: a person who designs buildings

design: to create the pattern or shape of something. Also, the pattern or shape of something.

evaluate: to determine the condition of

furnishing: an object used in a room or building

laundry: clothes to be washed

mansion: a big, fancy house

plaster: a paste that's used to coat walls

preserve: to keep something in its original state

renovation: the cleaning, repairing, or rebuilding of a building

retaliate: to return like for like

symbol: a picture or shape that stands for something else

FOR MORE INFORMATION

Books

Dillon, Patrick. *The Story of Buildings: From the Pyramids to the Sydney Opera House and Beyond.* Somerville, MA: Candlewick Press, 2014.

Slade, Suzanne. *The House That George Built.* Watertown, MA: Charlesbridge, 2012.

Wilson, Jon. *The White House.* Mankato, MN: Child's World, 2014.

Websites

Washington, DC Quick Facts for Kids
washington.org/DC-information/washington-dc-quick-facts-kids
Learn about our nation's capital here.

White House History: Facts
whitehousehistory.org/history/white-house-facts-trivia.html
Find out more cool facts about the White House and life there.

INDEX